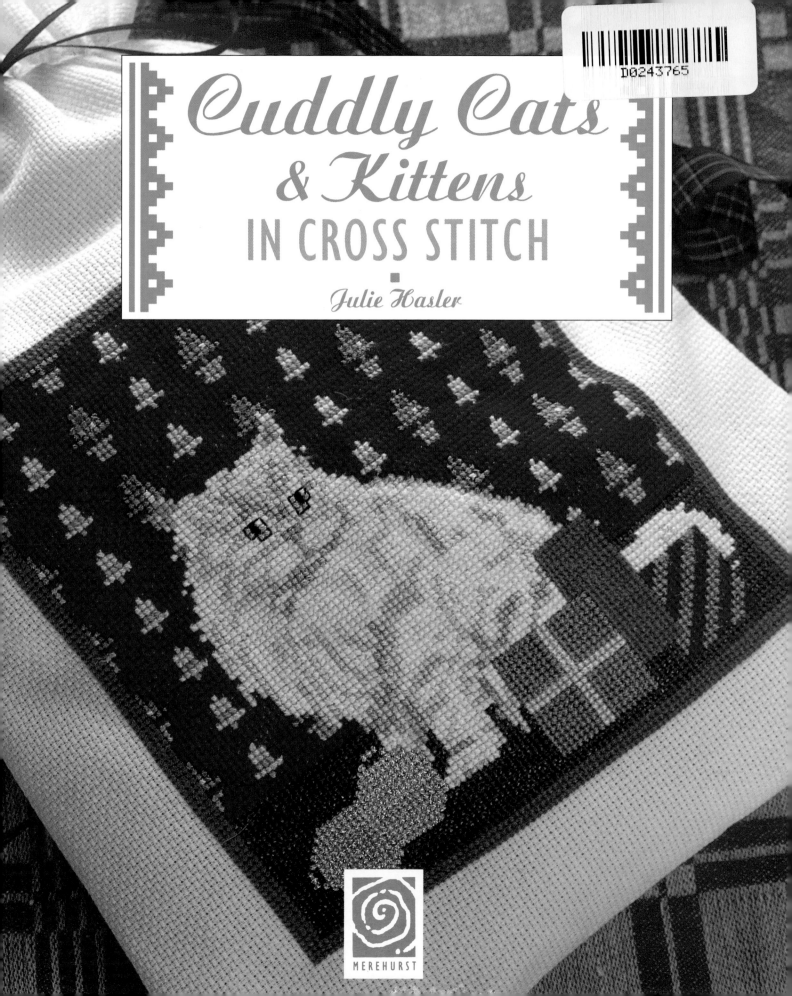

Cuddly Cats
& Kittens
IN CROSS STITCH

Julie Hasler

MEREHURST

THE CHARTS
Some of the designs in this book are very detailed and due to
inevitable space limitations, the charts may be shown on a
comparatively small scale; in such cases, readers may find it
helpful to have the particular chart with which they are
currently working enlarged.

THREADS
The projects in this book were all stitched with DMC stranded cotton
embroidery threads. The keys given with each chart also list thread
combinations for those who wish to use Anchor or Madeira threads.
It should be pointed out that the shades produced by different
companies vary slightly, and it is not always possible to find
identical colours in a different range.

Published in 1994 by Merehurst Limited
Ferry House, 51-57 Lacy Road, Putney, London SW15 1PR
Reprinted 1995
Text © Copyright 1994 Julie Hasler
Photography & illustrations © Copyright 1994 Merehurst Limited
ISBN 1 85391 387 1

A catalogue record for this book is available from the British Library.

Managing Editor Heather Dewhurst
Edited by Diana Lodge
Designed by Maggie Aldred
Photography by Marie-Louise Avery
Illustrations by John Hutchinson
Typesetting by BMD Graphics, Hemel Hempstead
Colour separation by Fotographics Limited, UK – Hong Kong
Printed in Hong Kong by Wing King Tong Co., Ltd.

*Merehurst is the leading publisher of craft books and has an excellent range
of titles to suit all levels. Please send to the address above for our
free catalogue, stating the title of this book.*

CONTENTS

INTRODUCTION

The favourite stitch of our great-grandmothers, cross stitch is becoming increasingly popular in these modern times for the decoration of household furnishings, linen and children's clothes. In fact, almost anything can lend itself to this type of embroidery, and what better subject can there be than the ever-popular cat? In this book, these two favourite themes are happily united, to offer a range of attractive and amusing projects which include cushions, photograph frames, tea towels, greetings cards, paperweights and much more.

Cross stitch is very easy to learn; there are only a few simple basic rules, and once you have mastered these, you can attempt any design. As with any craft, practice makes perfect, and you will find that perfection is quickly achieved.

Each cross stitch design is carefully charted and has an accompanying colour key and full instructions for making up the project. Also included is a Basic Skills section, which covers everything from how to prepare your fabric and stretch it in an embroidery hoop or frame, to mounting your cross stitch embroidery over card, ready for display.

Some of the designs are very simple and are aimed at beginners; others are more challenging, with many colours and shaded effects for the more experienced stitcher, or for those who are eager to expand their skills.

Whatever your level of skill or interest in the craft, you will enjoy being able to create items from the wide range of projects offered in this book, suitable for children and adults of all ages.

BASIC SKILLS

BEFORE YOU BEGIN

PREPARING THE FABRIC
Even with an average amount of handling, many evenweave fabrics tend to fray at the edges, so it is a good idea to overcast the raw edges, using ordinary sewing thread, before you begin.

THE INSTRUCTIONS
Each project begins with a full list of the materials that you will require; Aida, Tula, Lugana and Linda are all fabrics produced by Zweigart. Note that the measurements given for the embroidery fabric include a minimum of 3cm (1¼in) all around to allow for stretching it in a frame and preparing the edges to prevent them from fraying.

Colour keys for stranded embroidery cottons – DMC, Anchor or Madeira – are given with each chart. It is assumed that you will need to buy one skein of each colour mentioned in a particular key, even though you may use less, but where two or more skeins are needed, this information is included in the main list of requirements.

To work from the charts, particularly those where several symbols are used in close proximity, some readers may find it helpful to have the chart enlarged so that the squares and symbols can be seen more easily. Many photocopying services will do this for a minimum charge.

Before you begin to embroider, always mark the centre of the design with two lines of basting stitches, one vertical and one horizontal, running from edge to edge of the fabric, as indicated by the arrows on the charts.

As you stitch, use the centre lines given on the chart and the basting threads on your fabric as reference points for counting the squares and threads to position your design accurately.

WORKING IN A HOOP
A hoop is the most popular frame for use with small areas of embroidery. It consists of two rings, one fitted inside the other; the outer ring usually has an adjustable screw attachment so that it can be

tightened to hold the stretched fabric in place. Hoops are available in several sizes, ranging from 10cm (4in) in diameter to quilting hoops with a diameter of 38cm (15in). Hoops with table stands or floor stands attached are also available.

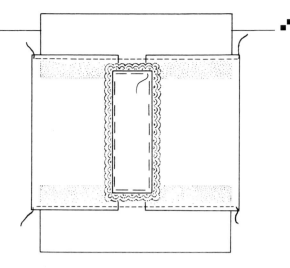

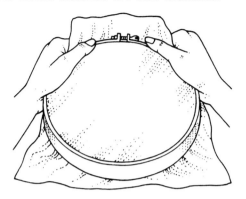

1 To stretch your fabric in a hoop, place the area to be embroidered over the inner ring and press the outer ring over it, with the tension screw released. Tissue paper can be placed between the outer ring and the embroidery, so that the hoop does not mark the fabric. Lay the tissue paper over the fabric when you set it in the hoop, then tear away the central embroidery area.

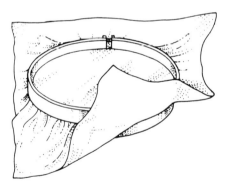

2 Smooth the fabric and, if necessary, straighten the grain before tightening the screw. The fabric should be evenly stretched.

EXTENDING EMBROIDERY FABRIC

It is easy to extend a piece of embroidery fabric, such as a bookmark, to stretch it in a hoop.

● Fabric oddments of a similar weight can be used. Simply cut four pieces to size (in other words, to the measurement that will fit both the embroidery fabric and your hoop) and baste them to each side of the embroidery fabric before stretching it in the hoop in the usual way.

WORKING IN A RECTANGULAR FRAME

Rectangular frames are more suitable for larger pieces of embroidery. They consist of two rollers, with tapes attached, and two flat side pieces, which slot into the rollers and are held in place by pegs or screw attachments. Available in different sizes, either alone or with adjustable table or floor stands, frames are measured by the length of the roller tape, and range in size from 30cm (12in) to 68cm (27in).

As alternatives to a slate frame, canvas stretchers and the backs of old picture frames can be used. Provided there is sufficient extra fabric around the finished size of the embroidery, the edges can be turned under and simply attached with drawing pins (thumb tacks) or staples.

1 To stretch your fabric in a rectangular frame, cut out the fabric, allowing at least an extra 5cm (2in) all around the finished size of the embroidery. Baste a single 12mm (½in) turning on the top and bottom edges and oversew strong tape, 2.5cm (1in) wide, to the other two sides. Mark the centre line both ways with basting stitches. Working from the centre outward and using strong thread, oversew the top and bottom edges to the roller tapes. Fit the side pieces into the slots, and roll any extra fabric on one roller until the fabric is taut.

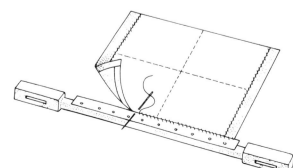

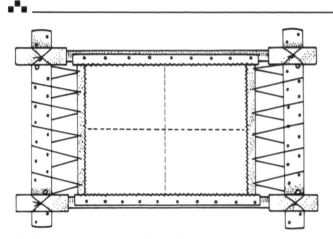

2 Insert the pegs or adjust the screw attachments to secure the frame. Thread a large-eyed needle (chenille needle) with strong thread or fine string and lace both edges, securing the ends around the intersections of the frame. Lace the webbing at 2.5cm (1in) intervals, stretching the fabric evenly.

ENLARGING A GRAPH PATTERN

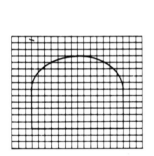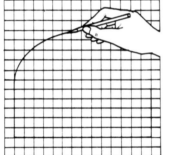

● To enlarge a graph pattern, you will need a sheet of graph paper ruled in 1cm (⅜in) squares, a ruler and pencil. If, for example, the scale is one square to 5cm (2in) you should first mark the appropriate lines to give a grid of the correct size. Copy the graph freehand from the small grid to the larger one, completing one square at a time. Use a ruler to draw the straight lines first, and then copy the freehand curves.

TO BIND AN EDGE

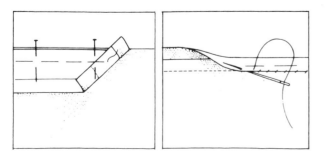

1 Open out the turning on one edge of the bias binding and pin in position on the right side of the fabric, matching the fold to the seamline. Fold over the cut end of the binding. Finish by overlapping the starting point by about 12mm (½in). Baste and machine stitch along the seam.
2 Fold the binding over the raw edge to the wrong side, baste and, using matching sewing thread, neatly hem to finish.

PIPED SEAMS

Contrasting piping adds a special decorative finish to a seam and looks particularly attractive on items such as cushions and cosies.

You can cover piping cord with either bias-cut fabric of your choice or a bias binding: alternatively, ready covered piping cord is available in several widths and many colours.

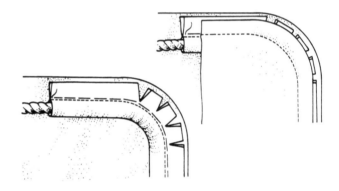

1 To apply piping, pin and baste it to the right side of the fabric, with seam lines matching. Clip into the seam allowance where necessary.
2 With right sides together, place the second piece of fabric on top, enclosing the piping. Baste and then either hand stitch in place or machine stitch, using a zipper foot. Stitch as close to the piping as possible, covering the first line of stitching.

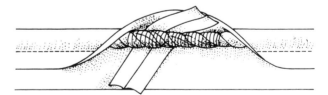

3 To join ends of piping cord together, first overlap the two ends by about 2.5cm (1in). Unpick the two cut ends of bias to reveal the cord. Join the bias strip as shown. Trim and press the seam open.
Unravel and slice the two ends of the cord. Fold the bias strip over it, and finish basting around the edge.

MOUNTING EMBROIDERY

The cardboard should be cut to the size of the finished embroidery, with an extra 6mm (½in) added all round to allow for the recess in the frame.

LIGHTWEIGHT FABRICS

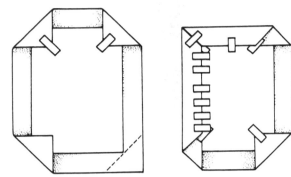

1 Place embroidery face down, with the cardboard centred on top, and basting and pencil lines matching. Begin by folding over the fabric at each corner and securing it with masking tape.

2 Working first on one side and then the other, fold over the fabric on all sides and secure it firmly with pieces of masking tape, placed about 2.5cm (1in) apart. Also neaten the mitred corners with masking tape, pulling the fabric tightly to give a firm, smooth finish.

HEAVIER FABRICS

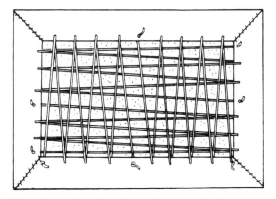

• Lay the embroidery face down, with the cardboard centred on top; fold over the edges of the fabric on opposite sides, making mitred folds at the corners, and lace across, using strong thread. Repeat on the other two sides. Finally, pull up the fabric firmly over the cardboard. Overstitch the mitred corners.

CROSS STITCH

For all cross stitch embroidery, the following two methods of working are used. In each case, neat rows of vertical stitches are produced on the back of the fabric.

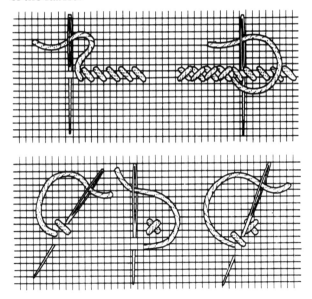

• When stitching large areas, work in horizontal rows. Working from right to left, complete the first row of evenly spaced diagonal stitches over the number of threads specified in the project instructions. Then, working from left to right, repeat the process. Continue in this way, making sure each stitch crosses in the same direction.
• When stitching diagonal lines, work downwards, completing each stitch before moving to the next.

BACKSTITCH

Backstitch is used in the projects to give emphasis to a particular foldline, an outline or a shadow. The stitches are worked over the same number of threads as the cross stitch, forming continuous straight or diagonal lines.

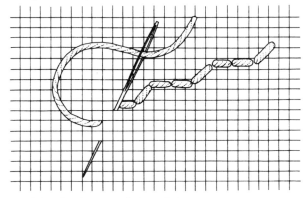

• Make the first stitch from left to right; pass the needle behind the fabric and bring it out one stitch length ahead to the left. Repeat and continue in this way along the line.

Lace-edged Cushions

These beautiful lace-edged cushions, with their amusing cartoon-style cats, are simple to make and will brighten up any child's room, either scattered on the bed, or on a favourite chair.

LACE-EDGED CUSHIONS

YOU WILL NEED

For each cushion, measuring 20cm (8in) square, excluding the lace edging:

*30cm (12in) square of white,
18-count Aida fabric
22.5cm (9in) of contrasting fabric to back
your cushion
2m (2¼yds) of white lace, 2.5cm (1in) deep
Stranded embroidery cotton in the colours given in
the panels
No26 tapestry needle
Sewing thread to match the fabric
A cushion pad, 21.5cm (8½in) square*

•

THE EMBROIDERY

Prepare the fabric, marking the centre lines of the design with basting stitches, and mount it in a hoop or frame, following the instructions on page 5. Referring to the appropriate chart, complete the cross stitching, starting at the centre and using two strands in the needle throughout. Embroider the main areas first, and then finish with the back-stitching, this time using a single strand in the needle. Steam press on the wrong side.

MAKING UP THE COVER

Trim the embroidery to measure 22.5cm (9in) square. Using a tiny french seam, join the short edges of the lace together. Run a gathering thread close to the straight edge; pull up the gathers to fit and, with the right side of the embroidery facing and the lace lying on the fabric, baste the edging to the outer edge, placing it just inside the 12mm (½in) seam allowance. Adjust the gathers evenly, allowing a little extra fullness at the corners. Machine stitch the frill in place.

With right sides together, place the backing fabric on top; baste and machine stitch around, leaving a 15cm (6in) opening in the middle of one side. Remove basting stitches; trim across the corners, and turn the cover through. Insert the cushion pad and slipstitch the opening to secure it.

SUMMER ▲		DMC	ANCHOR	MADEIRA
□	Bright canary yellow	973	290	0105
●	Dark royal blue	796	134	0914
Ⅱ	Red	666	46	0210
■	Dark golden brown	975	310	2303
Ⅰ	Light topaz yellow	726	295	0109
⋅	White	White	2	White
C	Pale grey	415	398	1803
O	Very light peach	948	778	0306
⊟	Light pumpkin orange	970	316	0204
⊠	Medium lavender	210	109	0803
◩	Black	310	403	Black
⊽	Medium peach	352	9	0303
	Peach*	353	8	0304
△	Light yellowy green	3348	264	1409

Note: outline eyes in black and nose and mouth in peach* (used for bks only).

WINTER ▼		DMC	ANCHOR	MADEIRA
☐	Dark grey	413	401	1713
⊡	Light grey	318	399	1802
⫿	Black	310	403	Black
☰	Very light avocado			
	green	472	264	1414
⧄	Dark forest green	986	245	1406
⊡	White	White	2	White
Ⓒ	Pale grey	415	398	1803
◹	Very light peach	948	778	0306
	Peach*	353	9	0304
☒	Medium peach	352	9	0303
⊙	Medium steel grey	317	400	1714
■	Very dark navy blue	939	152	1008
◪	Light yellowy green	3348	264	1409

Note: outline eyes in black and nose and mouth in peach* (used for bks only).

Photograph Frames

These delightful photograph frames will make an attractive addition to your home, whether displayed singly or together. Either of the two designs would make a lovely gift.

PHOTOGRAPH FRAMES

YOU WILL NEED

For the Butterfly Watcher frame, measuring 18cm (7in) approximately:

22.5cm (9in) square of white, 14-count Aida fabric
18cm (7in) square piece of mounting board

For the Cat and Mouse frame, measuring 24.5cm × 22.5cm (9¾in × 9in) approximately:

28cm × 25.5cm (11in × 10in) of white, 14-count Aida fabric
24.5cm × 22.5cm (9¾in × 9in) of mounting board

For each frame you will also need:

Stranded embroidery cotton in the colours given in the appropriate panel
No 24 tapestry needle
9cm (3½in) of white ribbon, 6mm (¼in) wide, for a hanging loop
Thin white card to back the frame
Masking tape
Craft adhesive
Scalpel or craft knife

•

THE EMBROIDERY

For each frame, prepare the fabric and stretch it in a hoop or frame (see pages 4-5). Embroider the border lines first, and then the rest of the design, using two strands of thread in the needle for cross stitching and one for the backstitching.

Leaving the basting stitches in at this stage, as guidelines, gently press the finished embroidery on the wrong side, using a steam iron.

MAKING THE FRAME

Carefully cut out a central window from the mounting board: the windows of the frames shown here measure 7cm × 6.5cm (2¾in × 2½in), but finished embroideries can vary slightly in size, so check your own inner frame measurement.

Place your embroidery face down on a firm, flat surface and, using the basting stitches as a guide, position the mounting board on top of it. Next, mark the cut-out on the fabric with a soft pencil. Remove the basting stitches and, using a sharp pair of scissors, make a small nick in the centre of the fabric, and cut diagonally from the centre up to each marked corner. Place the mounting board over the fabric again, and fold the triangles of fabric to the back of the board, securing them with masking tape. Next, fold in the outer edges of fabric, mitring the corners and securing them with tape (see page 7).

Using tape or craft adhesive, secure your chosen photograph in position. Form the ribbon into a loop, and secure it to the back of the frame with adhesive, then cut a piece of white card to neaten the back of the frame and secure this also with adhesive.

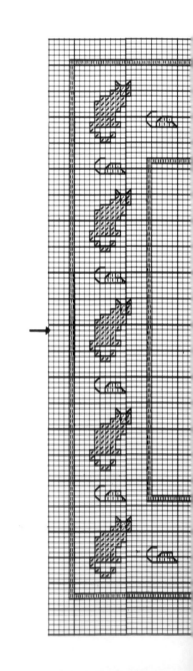

CAT AND MOUSE ▼		DMC	ANCHOR	MADEIRA
	Black*	310	403	Black
ⅠⅠ	Dark delft blue	798	146	0911
▪	Peach	351	10	0214
▪∴	White	White	2	White
◪	Medium old gold	729	890	2210
ⅠⅠ	Pale grey	415	398	1803

Note: bks outlines in grey and make eyes with french knots in black* (used for this only).

BUTTERFLY WATCHER ▼		DMC	ANCHOR	MADEIRA
	Black*	310	403	Black
ⅠⅠ	Very light carnation red	894	26	0413
▪	Peach	353	9	0304
▪∴	White	White	2	White
◪	Medium old gold	729	890	2210
	Steel grey*	414	400	1801

Note: bks outlines in steel grey* (used for bks only) and make eyes with french knots in black* (used for this only).

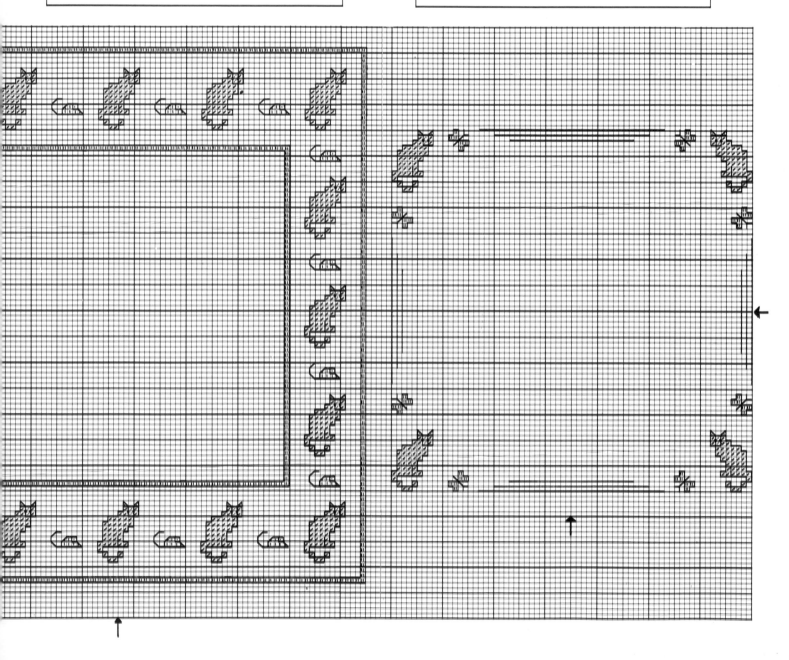

Kitten Paperweights

These beautiful paperweights make gifts which are both useful and decorative. They can be used to adorn a desk, a small table or even a mantelpiece.

KITTEN PAPERWEIGHTS

YOU WILL NEED

For each paperweight, Sleepy Kitten, an oval measuring 9.5cm × 6cm (3⅝in × 2⅜in); Puss in Boot, measuring 6.7cm (2⅝in) in diameter, and Hat Cat, a heart-shape measuring 6.5cm × 6cm (2½ × 2¼in):

15cm (6in) square of white, 25-count Lugana fabric
Stranded embroidery cotton in the colours given in the appropriate panel
No26 tapestry needle
Paperweight (for suppliers, see page 48)

•

THE EMBROIDERY

Each of these designs is stitched in the same way and on the same type of fabric. If you wish to embroider all three, you may be able to economize on fabric by using one large piece, remembering to allow sufficient space between each design.

Prepare the fabric and set it in a hoop (see pages 4-5). Complete the cross stitch embroidery, using one strand of thread in the needle throughout, and taking each stitch over one fabric intersection.

Gently press the finished embroidery on the wrong side.

ASSEMBLING THE PAPERWEIGHT

Place the embroidery face up on a firm, flat surface and use the paper template (provided with the paperweight) to draw around your design, ensuring that it is central. Cut the fabric to size and place right side down into the recess on the base of the paperweight. Place the paper template on to the reverse side of your embroidery. Next, peel the backing off the protective base and very carefully stick it to the base of the paperweight, ensuring that the embroidery and template do not move out of place.

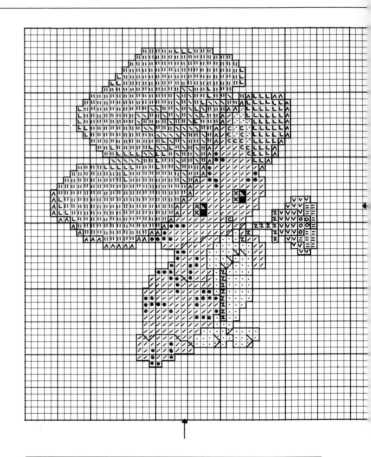

HAT CAT ▲		DMC	ANCHOR	MADEIRA
∧	Very dark cranberry	600	65	0704
∟	Medium cranberry	602	62	0702
‖	Light cranberry	604	60	0614
＼	Dark delft blue	798	131	0911
⊙	Yellow	727	293	0110
⊟	Very light dusky rose	963	73	0502
∨	Rose pink	962	52	0609
Z	Medium avocado green	3347	267	1408
C	Medium peach	352	9	0303
∙	Light peach	754	6	0305
／	Very light beaver grey	3072	847	1805
●	Medium grey	414	400	1801
	Dark grey*	413	401	1713
⊠	Light yellowy green	3348	264	1409
⊡	White	White	2	White
■	Black	310	403	Black

Note: bks outline in dark grey (used for outlines only).*

SLEEPY KITTEN ▶	DMC	ANCHOR	MADEIRA
■ Black	310	403	Black
☒ Light yellowy green	3348	264	1409
• White	White	2	White
◉ Medium grey	414	400	1801
⌿ Very light beaver grey	3072	847	1805
⦂ Light peach	754	6	0305
C Medium peach	352	9	0303
⬉ Very light pearl grey	762	397	1804
⫴ Red	666	46	0210
Dark grey*	413	401	1713

Note: bks outlines in dark grey* (used for outlines only).

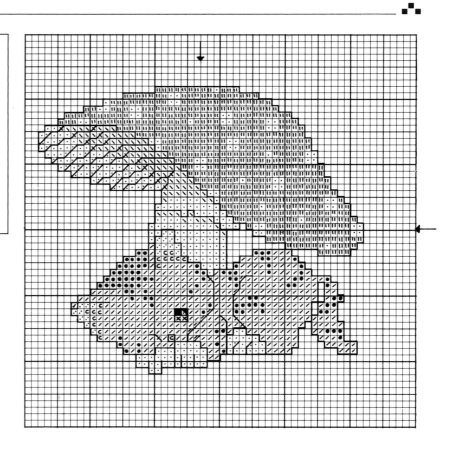

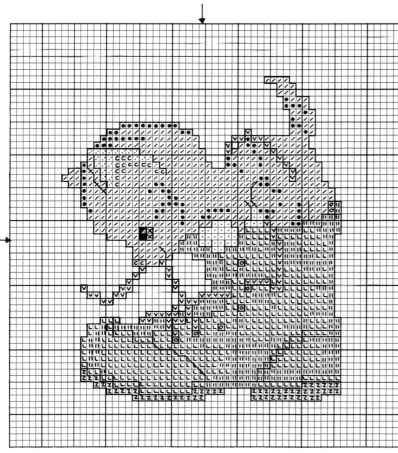

PUSS IN BOOT ◀	DMC	ANCHOR	MADEIRA
☒ Light yellowy green	3348	264	1409
■ Black	310	403	Black
• White	White	2	White
⦂ Light peach	754	6	0305
C Medium peach	352	9	0303
◉ Medium grey	415	398	1803
Very dark grey*	413	401	1713
⌿ Very light beaver grey	3072	847	1805
⋁ Golden wheat	3046	887	2102
⤢ Brown grey	3022	392	1903
⌐ Very light tan	738	942	2013
⫴ Medium brown	433	371	2008
O Very dark coffee brown	898	380	2007

Note: bks outlines in very dark grey* (used for bks only).

Knitting Bag

This useful knitting bag makes an extremely practical gift for any keen knitter or craft enthusiast. The bag is sufficiently large and strong to hold most on-going craft projects, including embroideries and patchwork projects as well as knitting, and the playful kittens are sure to thrill any cat lover.

KNITTING BAG

YOU WILL NEED

For each Knitting bag, measuring
36.5cm × 32cm (14½in × 12½in):

*42cm × 76cm (16½in × 30in) of cream,
14-count Aida fabric
42cm × 76cm (16½in × 30in) of thin
polyester batting
42cm × 76cm (16½in × 30in) of calico,
for the lining
Stranded embroidery cotton in the colours given in
the panel
No 24 tapestry needle
Sewing thread to match the fabric
A pair of handles (for suppliers, see page 48)*

•

THE EMBROIDERY

Fold the embroidery fabric in half; press and unfold. Taking the top (bag front) section, mark the centre lines with basting stitches (see page 4) and set it in a frame. Complete the cross stitching, using two strands of thread in the needle, and then the backstitching, using one strand. Ensure that there is approximately 9cm (3½in) clearance at each side of the finished embroidery (front section), 2.5cm (1in) at the bottom, and 12.5cm (5in) at the top.

Gently steam press the embroidered fabric on the wrong side.

MAKING THE BAG

Pin, baste and stitch the batting to the wrong side of the embroidered fabric, stitching around all sides and taking a 1cm (½in) seam allowance. Trim the batting back to the stitching line. Fold the fabric in half, with right sides facing, and pin and baste the side seams, taking a 1cm (½in) seam allowance Stitch the side seams, stopping 16.5cm (6½in) short of the top edge at each side.

Fold the lining in half, with right sides facing, and stitch the side seams, as for the main fabric. Turn the main fabric right side out and place the lining inside the bag. Turn in the 12mm (½in) allowance around the remaining raw edges and top stitch them together, making sure that no lining is visible on the right side. Thread the top edges of the bag through the bag handles, gathering the fabric evenly, and catch-stitch by hand to finish.

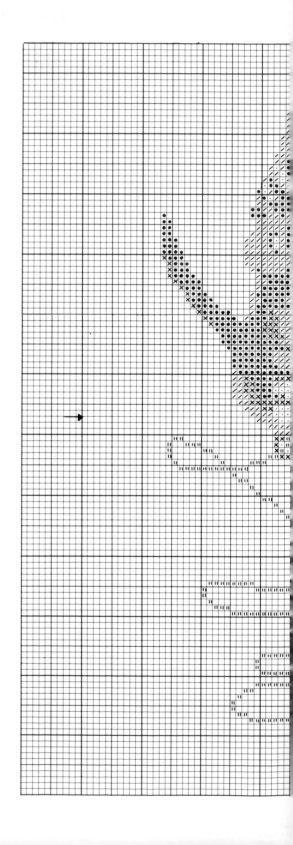

KNITTING BAG ▼	DMC	ANCHOR	MADEIRA
● Dark steel grey	413	401	1713
✕ Steel grey	414	400	1801
╱ Pale grey	415	398	1803
• White	White	2	White
‖ Medium pink	899	27	0505

Note: bks outline in pale grey.

Three in a Row

This delightful picture with its trio of irresistible kittens would certainly win the heart of any cat lover, and brighten up any room in the house. The subtle shading makes it an enjoyable challenge for the more experienced cross stitch enthusiast.

THREE IN A ROW

YOU WILL NEED

For the picture, measuring 42cm × 37cm
(16½in × 14½in) unframed:

*50cm × 45cm (20in × 18in) of cream, 28-count
Quaker cloth
Stranded embroidery cotton in the colours given in
the panel
No 26 tapestry needle
42cm × 37cm (16½in × 14½in) of mounting
board
Picture frame of your choice*

•

THE EMBROIDERY

Prepare the fabric and stretch it in a frame (see
page 5). Following the chart, start the embroidery
at the centre of the design, using two strands of
thread in the needle and making each cross stitch
over two fabric threads. Finish by backstitching
around the eyes, using one strand of thread in
the needle.

Leaving the basting stitches in position, gently
steam press the finished embroidery on the wrong
side.

MOUNTING

You can use either of the methods described
on page 7 to mount your finished embroidery. To
achieve a smooth finish, you may find that it is
helpful to secure the fabric to one edge of the board
with pins, working from the centre point out to both
corners, and then repeat for the opposite side, to
make sure that the fabric is even and taut. Secure
with tape or lacing, and then repeat for the remaining sides.

If you are setting the mounted fabric in the frame
yourself, use rustproof pins to secure the backing
board, and seal the back of the picture with broad
tape, to ensure that dust cannot enter the frame.

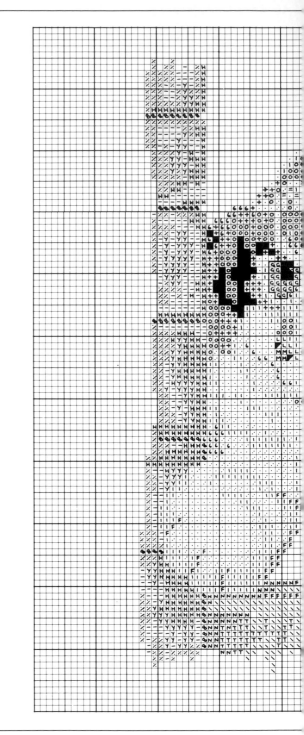

FRAMED PICTURE ▲	DMC	ANCHOR	MADEIRA
■ Black	310	403	Black
G Khaki	733	280	1611
• White	White	2	White
☒ Dark mahogany brown	300	352	2304
☐ Peach	353	8	0304
M Medium peach	352	9	0303
◪ Brick red	355	5968	0401
‖ Medium mahogany brown	301	370	2306
Z Light old gold	676	891	2208
𝟨 Dark pewter grey	535	401	1809

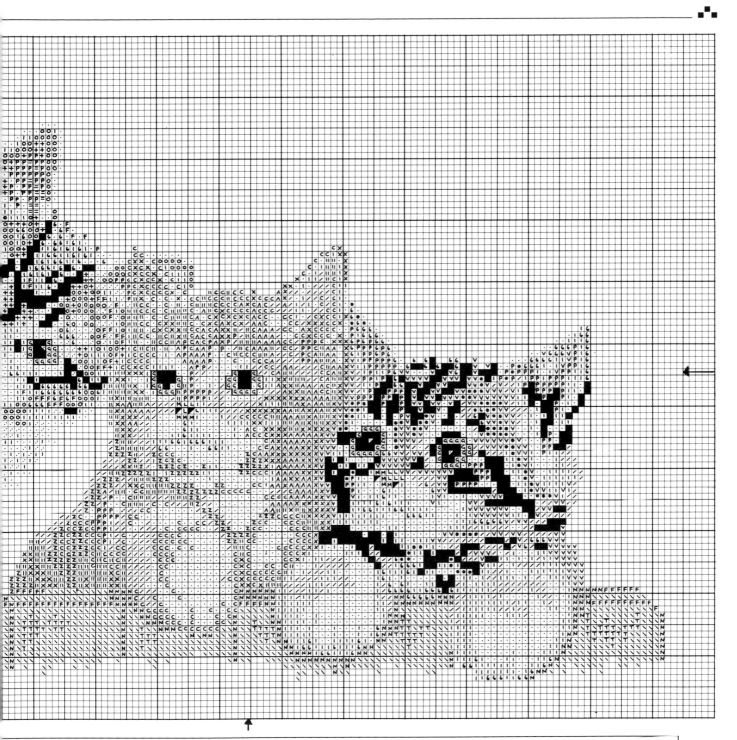

		DMC	ANCHOR	MADEIRA			DMC	ANCHOR	MADEIRA
I	Pale grey	415	398	1803	+	Medium beaver grey	647	399	1812
/	Light khaki green	3013	853	2110	%	Light antique pink	950	376	2309
V	Light brown grey	3023	1040	1903	−	Pale brick red	758	868	0403
C	Medium beige grey	644	392	1902	Y	Medium brick red	356	339	0402
P	Very light beige brown	842	376	1910	H	Brick red	355	5968	0401
●	Brown grey	3022	392	1812	⦿	Very dark brown grey	3021	905	1904
∧	Medium old gold	729	890	2210	N	Medium steel grey	317	400	1714
.·	Very light pearl grey	762	397	1804	\	Pale blue grey	928	900	1709
F	Light steel grey	318	399	1802	T	Light antique blue	932	1033	1710
O	Light beaver grey	648	900	1814					
=	Shell grey	451	233	1808		*Note: bks around eyes in black.*			

Greetings Cards

Personalized greetings cards containing a small embroidery are a pleasure to make or to receive. Here are three lovely caricature cat designs, one for Christmas, one to offer congratulations (perhaps for an 18th or 21st birthday, an engagement or an anniversary) and a Valentine's Day card.

GREETINGS CARDS

YOU WILL NEED

For each card, measuring 15.5cm × 11cm
(6¼in × 14⅜in):

*19cm × 15cm (7½in × 6in) of white, 22-count
Hardanger fabric
Stranded embroidery cotton in the colours
given in the appropriate panel
No 26 tapestry needle
Double-sided adhesive tape
Iron-on interfacing (optional, see Making up the
cards) – 12mm (½in) larger all around than the
size of the inner frame of your chosen card.
Card mount (for suppliers, see page 48),
as appropriate:
Cat's Christmas – holly green with a
rectangular cut-out
Champagne Charlies – pale blue with an
oval cut-out
Valentine's Day – Christmas red with an
oval cut-out*

•

THE EMBROIDERY

Each of these designs is stitched in the same way
and on the same type of fabric. If you wish to
embroider all three, you may be able to economize
on fabric by using one large piece, remembering to
allow sufficient space between each design.

Note that it is particularly important with
embroidered cards to avoid excessive overstitching
on the back, as this would cause unsightly lumps
to show through on the right side.

Prepare the fabric, marking the centre lines of
each design with basting stitches, and mount it in
a small hoop, following the instructions on page 5.
Referring to the appropriate chart, complete the
cross stitching, using a single strand in the needle
throughout. Embroider the main areas first, and
then finish with the backstitching. If necessary,
steam press on the wrong side.

It is a good idea to leave the basting stitches in
at this stage, as they will prove useful in helping to
centre your design in the card window.

MAKING UP THE CARDS

It is not strictly necessary to use iron-on interfacing,
but it helps to avoid wrinkles. If you are using

interfacing, place it on the back of the embroidery;
use a pencil to mark the basting/registration points
on the interfacing and outer edge of the embroidery.
Remove basting stitches and iron the interfacing in
place, aligning marks.

Trim the embroidery to about 12mm (½in) larger
than the cut-out window, and then, making sure
that the motif is placed in the middle by measuring an equal distance at each side of the marks,
position the embroidery behind the window. Use
double-sided tape to fix the embroidery into the
card, then press the backing down firmly.

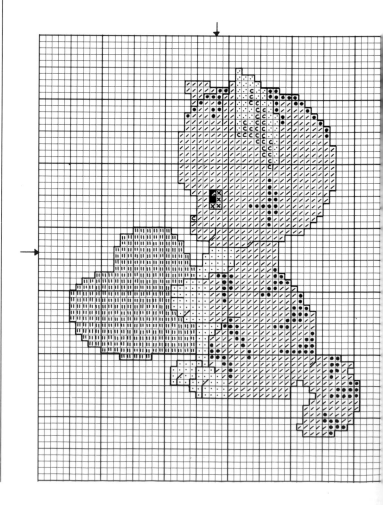

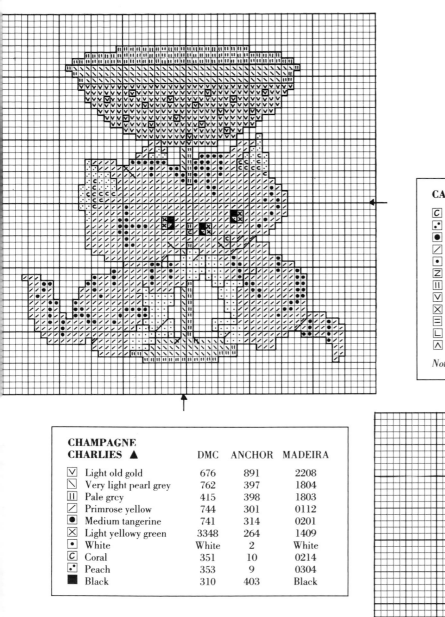

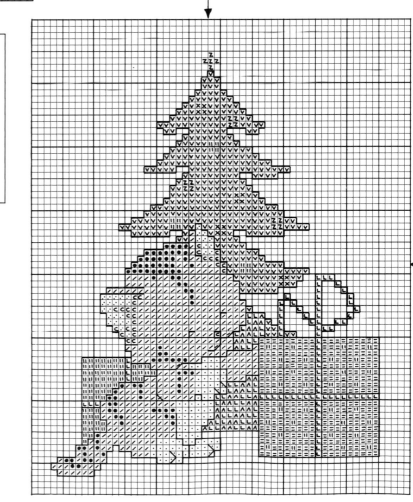

CAT'S CHRISTMAS ▼		DMC	ANCHOR	MADEIRA
C	Coral	351	10	0214
⦂	Peach	353	9	0304
●	Medium tangerine	741	314	0201
╱	Primrose yellow	744	301	0112
•	White	White	2	White
Z	Silver thread			
‖	Red	666	46	0210
V	Christmas green	700	228	1305
X	Gold thread			
=	Apple green	702	239	1306
L	Old gold	725	306	0108
∧	Mauve	333	111	0903

Note: bks outlines in black.

CHAMPAGNE CHARLIES ▲		DMC	ANCHOR	MADEIRA
V	Light old gold	676	891	2208
╲	Very light pearl grey	762	397	1804
‖	Pale grey	415	398	1803
╱	Primrose yellow	744	301	0112
●	Medium tangerine	741	314	0201
X	Light yellowy green	3348	264	1409
•	White	White	2	White
C	Coral	351	10	0214
⦂	Peach	353	9	0304
■	Black	310	403	Black

VALENTINE'S DAY ◀		DMC	ANCHOR	MADEIRA
•	White	White	2	White
X	Light yellowy green	3348	264	1409
‖	Red	666	46	0210
╱	Primrose yellow	744	301	0112
●	Medium tangerine	741	314	0201
C	Coral	351	10	0214
⦂	Peach	353	9	0304
■	Black	310	403	Black

Gift Bag

This pretty gift bag is just the right size to hold a small gift, and can be used afterwards to hold handkerchiefs or jewellery. It is the perfect way to make a present extra special.

GIFT BAG

YOU WILL NEED

For each Gift bag, measuring 32cm × 22cm
(12½in × 8¾in):

*32.5cm × 76cm (13in × 30½in) of white,
16-count Aida fabric
1.12m (44in) of red ribbon, 2.5mm (⅛in) wide
Stranded embroidery cotton in the colours given in
the panel
Metallic threads in gold and silver
No 24 tapestry needle
Sewing thread to match the fabric*

•

THE EMBROIDERY

Using the diagram as a guide, and bearing in mind
that there is an additional 3cm (1¼in) of fabric all
around to allow for fraying, mark out the embroidery area with basting stitches, setting it 18cm
(7¼in) down from the raw top edge of the fabric.
Mark the centre lines of the embroidery area with
basting stitches and set it in a hoop or frame (see
pages 4-5). Working from the centre, complete
the cross stitch embroidery, using two strands of
embroidery cotton in the needle. Finish by working
the backstitching, using one strand in the needle.

Gently steam press the finished embroidery on
the wrong side.

MAKING THE BAG

Trim the fabric to measure 25.5cm × 70cm (10¼in
× 28in). Using a blunt-tipped needle, remove two
threads from the top and bottom of the fabric,
7.5cm (3in) in from the raw edge, as marked on the
diagram. Fold your embroidery in half, with right
sides together; pin and baste the side seams, then
either machine stitch or sew the sides by hand,
taking a 12mm (½in) seam allowance and stopping
2cm (¾in) from the top.

Trim diagonally across the bottom corners to
remove excess fabric and turn the bag right side
out. Beginning at the centre front of the bag, weave
the ribbon through the loops made by removing the
threads. You may find this easier if you thread the
ribbon onto a large blunt-tipped tapestry needle.
Finally, make the fringe for the top of the bag by
removing the fabric threads one at a time, fraying

the fabric for 2cm (¾in) down to the side seam
stitching. Brush the fringe out afterwards with a
stiff brush.

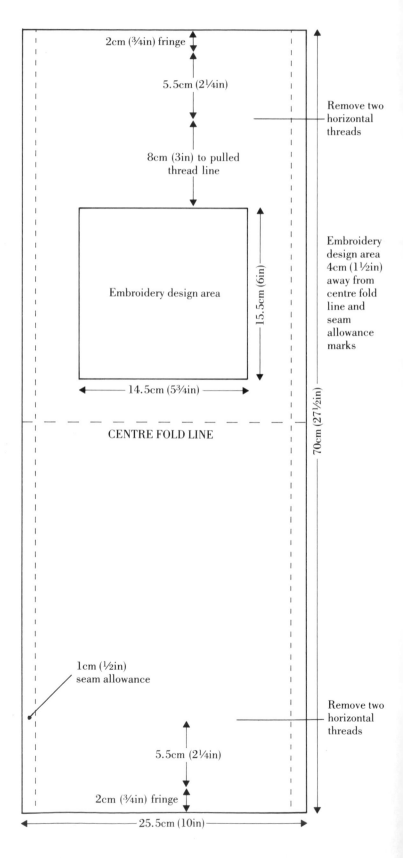

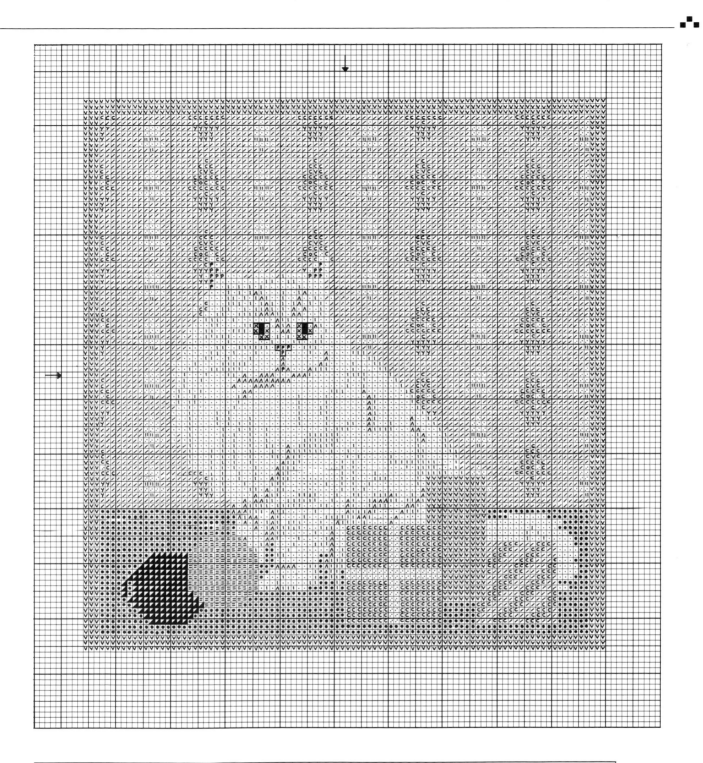

GIFT BAG ▲		DMC	ANCHOR	MADEIRA			DMC	ANCHOR	MADEIRA
■	Black	310	403	Black	△	Pale grey	415	398	1803
•	White	White	2	White	▤	Silver thread			
I	Very light pearl grey	762	397	1804	•⦂	Light topaz yellow	726	295	0109
C	Medium emerald green	911	205	1214	II	Gold	783	307	2211
	Light salmon pink*	761	8	0404	●	Dark royal blue	796	134	0914
V	Very dark lavender	208	111	0804	◪	Gold thread			
X	Light avocado green	471	266	1501					
／	Red	666	46	0210	*Note: outline nose in salmon pink* and eyes in medium steel*				
⊙	Medium electric blue	996	433	1103	*grey* (both used for bks outline only).*				
	Medium steel grey*	414	400	1801					

Serving Tray

When guests call in for morning coffee or afternoon tea, enchant them with this delightful tray – beautifully embroidered and mounted under glass. Alternatively, the design could be used for a small picture or a scatter cushion.

SERVING TRAY

YOU WILL NEED

For the tray, measuring 30.5cm × 40.5cm
(12in × 16in) with a 23cm × 30.5cm
(9in × 12in) oval cut-out:

*38cm × 48cm (15in × 19in) of pink, 14-count
Aida fabric
Stranded embroidery cotton in the colours given in
the panel
No 24 tapestry needle
Serving tray (for suppliers, see page 48)*

•

THE EMBROIDERY

Prepare the fabric and set it in a hoop or frame (see pages 4-5). Complete the cross stitch embroidery, using two strands of thread in the needle throughout. Finish by backstitching around the eyes, using one strand of black in the needle.

Gently steam press the finished embroidery on the wrong side.

ASSEMBLING THE TRAY

Gently remove all parts from the tray, following the manufacturer's instructions. Using a soft pencil, mark the supplied mounting board both ways along the centre to help you to position the board exactly in the middle of your embroidery. Place the embroidery face down on a firm, flat surface, and place the mounting board centrally on top. Fold the edges of the fabric over the board on all four sides, working first on one side and then the opposite side. Secure with one piece of masking tape on each side. When you are sure that the design is centred, turn in each corner to form a mitre, and secure firmly with masking tape. Next, finish securing the sides in the same way, ensuring that the fabric is stretched evenly. Insert the mounted embroidery into the tray, following the manufacturer's instructions.

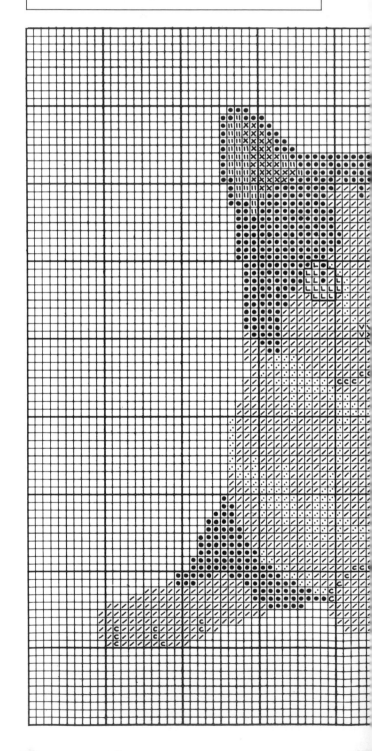

TRAY ▼		DMC	ANCHOR	MADEIRA
●	Black	310	403	Black
╱	White	White	2	White
•ˑ	Pale grey	415	398	1803
C	Light steel grey	318	399	1802
II	Steel grey	414	400	1801
V	Light antique pink	950	376	2309
X	Pale brick red	758	868	0403
L	Light yellowy green	3348	264	1409

Note: use black to outline eyes.

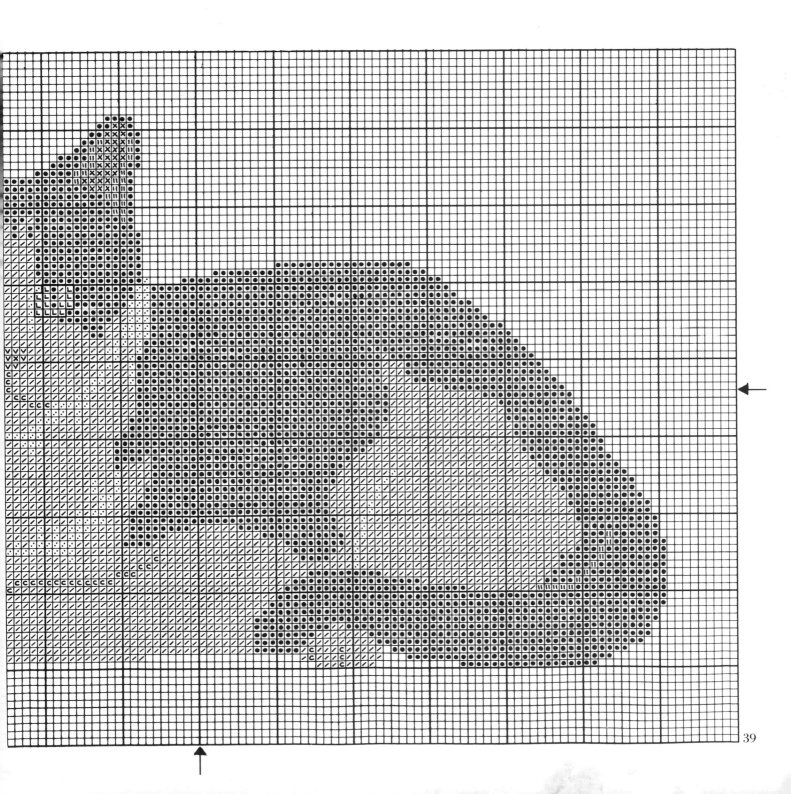

Tea Towels

The fabric used for these delightful tea towels has a reversible design and evenweave strips, intended for cross stitching, at both ends.
It is the width of two tea towels.

TEA TOWELS

YOU WILL NEED

For a pair of tea towels, each measuring
77.5cm × 45cm (30in × 18in):

50cm (19⅝in) of Zweigart 'Cats' fabric
Stranded embroidery cotton in the colours given in
the panel
No 24 tapestry needle
Sewing thread to match the fabric

•

THE EMBROIDERY

Fold and press the fabric to mark the dividing line
between the two tea towels, and cut along the foldline. Prepare the fabric (see page 4), marking the
centre point with a line of basting stitches across
the cross stitch band.

For each towel, set the fabric in a hoop or frame
(see pages 4-5). Complete the cross stitch embroidery, using three strands of embroidery cotton in the
needle throughout, and taking each stitch over one
fabric intersection. Finish with the backstitching,
this time using two strands of thread in the needle.
The repeats should stop 12mm (½in) short of the
raw edge at each side, to allow for the hem.

Gently press the finished embroidery on the
wrong side.

FINISHING THE TEA TOWELS

Pin and tack a 7mm (¼in) double hem on all four
sides. Machine stitch all around for a secure finish.

The border patterns have been designed with
mix-and-match in mind, so experiment with vari-
ations, interspersing the CATS lettering with paws,
for example, to make as many tea towels as you
wish.

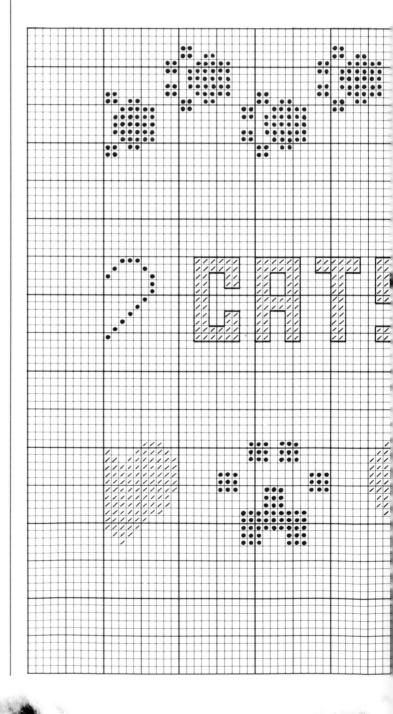

CATS ▼		DMC	ANCHOR	MADEIRA
⬤ Black		310	403	Black
⧄ Red		666	46	0210

Note: bks outline in black.

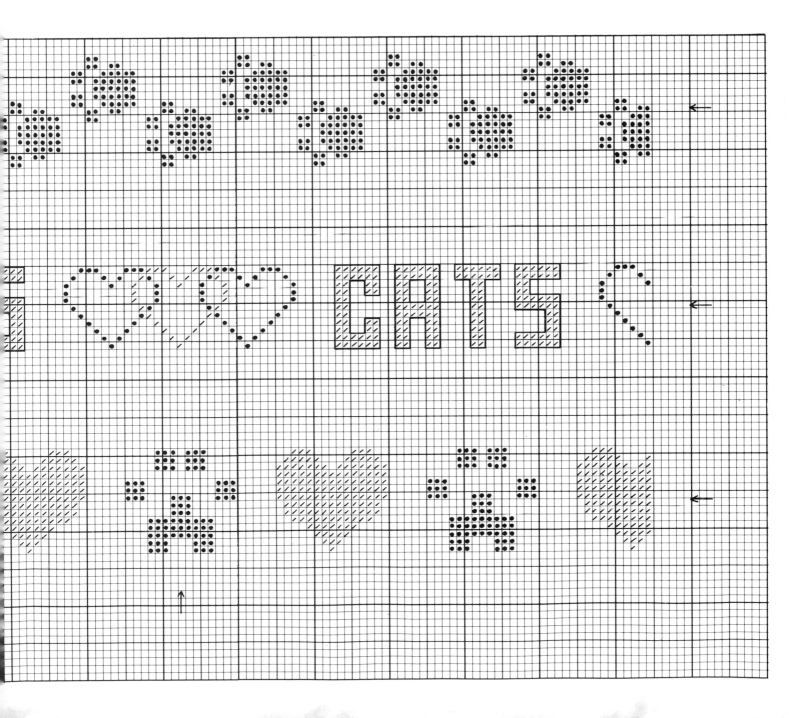

Nightdress Case

Make this luxurious case to tuck away your nightie or pyjamas during the day. Lightly padded, trimmed with ribbon bows, and featuring a sleeping cat, it will look beautiful sitting on top of any bed.

NIGHTDRESS CASE

YOU WILL NEED

For a nightdress case, measuring 45cm × 33cm (17¾in × 13in):

*94cm × 46.5cm (37in × 18½in) of pink,
14-count Aida fabric
94cm × 46.5cm (37in × 18½in) of lightweight
polyester batting
94cm × 46.5cm (37in × 18½in) of lightweight
cotton fabric for the lining
1.12m (44in) of ribbon, 2.5cm (1in) wide, in a
contrast colour
Stranded embroidery cotton in the colours given in
the panel
No 24 tapestry needle
Sewing thread to match the fabric*

•

THE EMBROIDERY

Prepare the edges of the fabric (see page 4); baste a line across the width, 7.5cm (3in) up from the bottom edge, to mark the baseline of the embroidery, and another 28.5cm (11½in) up from the bottom edge (this marks off the area for the front flap), then baste horizontal and vertical lines across the embroidery area in the usual way.

Complete the cross stitching, working from the centre and using two strands of embroidery thread in the needle. Finish with the backstitching, made with one thread in the needle. Gently steam press the embroidery from the wrong side.

MAKING THE NIGHTDRESS CASE

Place the embroidered fabric face down on a flat surface; carefully smooth the batting on top; pin and baste the two together (12mm/½in seam allowance); trim the batting back almost to the basting line, and catch-stitch around the edge.

Make a single 12mm (½in) turning across the width (not flap edge) of the fabric and baste. With right sides facing, fold the pocket front section over for 32cm (12½in); baste, and machine stitch to form the pocket. Trim the corners and turn right side out.

Make a single turning on the short edge of the lining fabric and repeat as for the top fabric, but do not turn the pocket to the right side.

With right sides of the top fabric and lining together, baste and stitch around the flap, finishing just above the side seams. Trim the corners and turn the flap through to the right side. Slip the lining into the pocket and slipstitch the top edges together, easing the turning so that the stitching is on the inside. Remove the basting stitches.

Cut the ribbon into two equal lengths; make two bows and catch-stitch them to the flap of the nightdress case diagonally across the corners, as shown in the photograph.

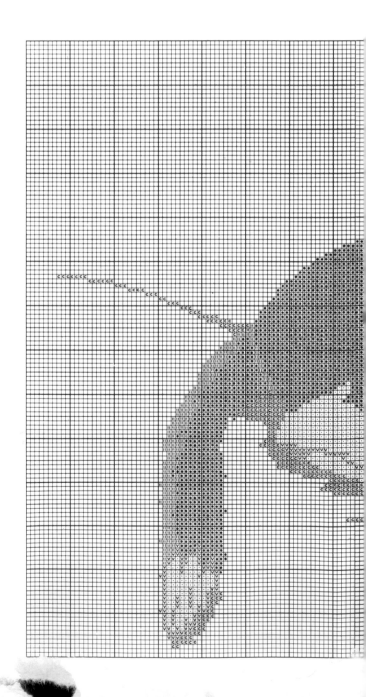

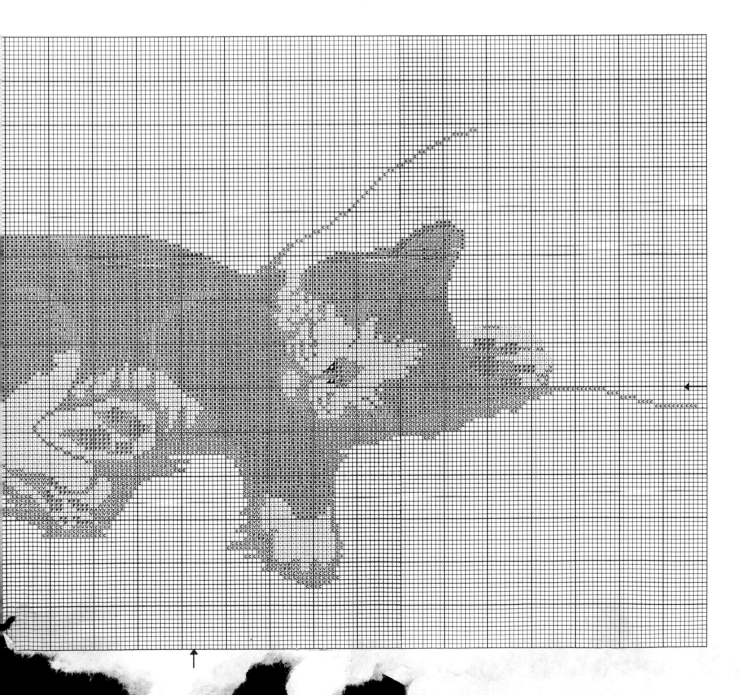

ACKNOWLEDGEMENTS

The Author would like to thank the following people for their help with this book:

For the embroidery work: Odette Robinson, Allison Mortley, Linda Potter, Barbara Hodgkinson, Jenny Whitlock, Libby Shaw, Lesley Buckerfield and Dawn Parmley.

For making up the projects: Louise Wells.

For supplying items and fabrics for use in this book: DMC Creative World Ltd (*for the fabrics, threads and DMC items*) and Framecraft Miniatures Ltd (*paperweight and tray*). Both suppliers request that a stamped self-addressed envelope be enclosed with all enquiries.

SUPPLIERS

The following mail order company has supplied some of the basic items needed for making up the projects in this book:

Framecraft Miniatures Limited
372/376 Summer Lane
Hockley
Birmingham, B19 3QA
England
Telephone (021) 359 4442

Addresses for Framecraft stockists worldwide
Ireland Needlecraft Pty. Ltd.
2-4 Keppel Drive
Hallam, Victoria 3803
Australia

Danish Art Needlework
PO Box 442, Lethbridge
Alberta T1J 3Z1
Canada

Sanyei Imports
PO Box 5, Hash   i
Gifu 501-6

The Embroidery Shop
286 Queen Street
Masterton
New Zealand

Anne Brinkley Designs Inc.
246 Walnut Street
Newton
Mass. 02160
USA

S A Threads and Cottons Ltd.
43 Somerset Road
Cape Town
South Africa

For information on your nearest stockist of embroidery cotton, contact the following:

DMC

UK
DMC Creative World Limited
62 Pullman Road
Wigston
Leicester, LE8 2DY
.hone: 0533 81104

USA
The DMC Corporation
Port Kearney Bld.
10 South Kearney
N.J. 07032-0650
Telephone: 201 589 0606

AUSTRALIA
DMC Needlecraft Pty
P.O. Box 317
Earlswood 2206
NSW 2204
Telephone: 02599 3088

COATS AND ANCHOR

UK
Kilncraigs Mill
Alloa
Clackmannanshire
Scotland, FK10 1EG
Telephone: 0259 723431

USA
Coats & Clark
P.O. Box 27067
Dept CO1
Greenville
SC 29616
.lephone: 803   ·4 0103

AUSTRALIA
Coats Patons Crafts
Thistle Street
Launceston
Tasmania 7250
Telephone: 00344 4222

MADEIRA

UK
Madeira Threads (UK) Limited
Thirsk Industrial Park
York Road, Thirsk
N. Yorkshire, YO7 3BX
Telephone: 0845 524880

USA
Madeira Marketing Limited
600 East 9th Street
Michigan City
IN 46360
Telephone: 219 873 1000

AUSTRALIA
Penguin Threads Pty Limitec
25-27 Izett Street
Prahran
Victoria 3181
Telephone: (